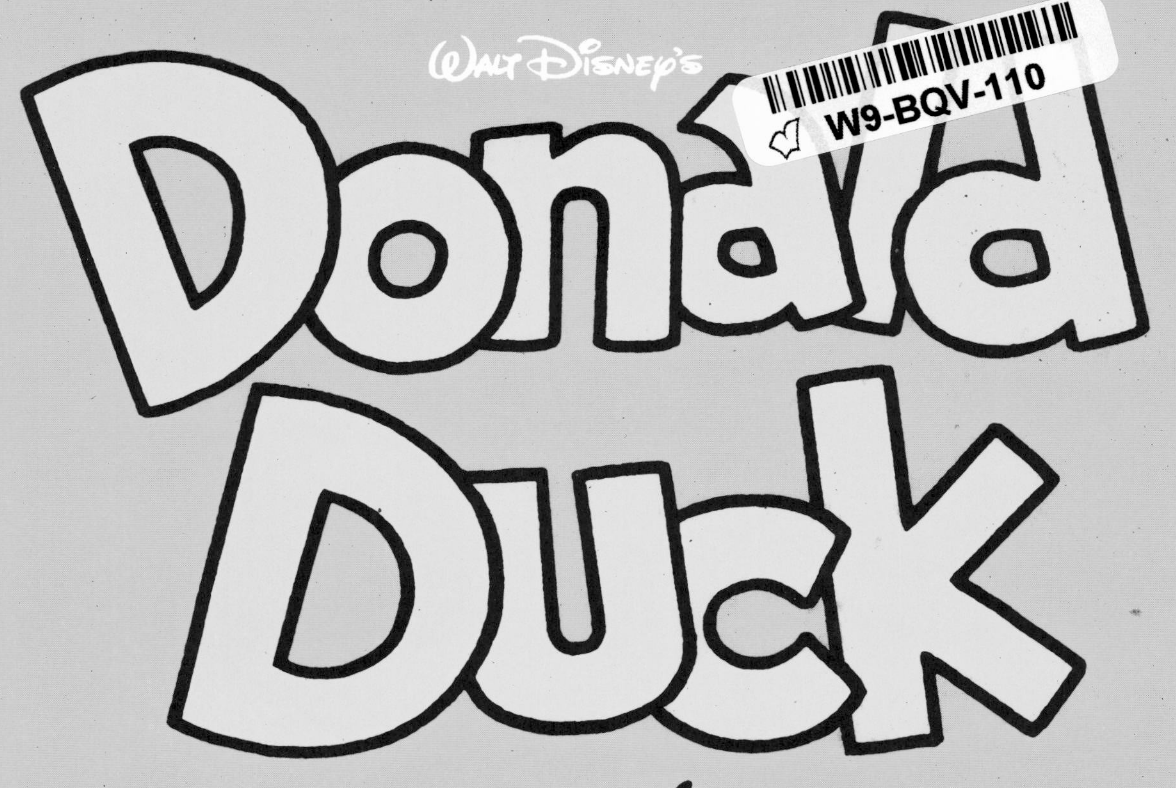

and the...

Executive Editor: Gary Groth

Senior Editor: J. Michael Catron

Colorist: Rich Tommaso

Designer: Keeli McCarthy

Production: Paul Baresh

Associate Publisher: Eric Reynolds

Publisher: Gary Groth

Fantagraphics Books, Inc.
7563 Lake City Way NE
Seattle, WA 98115

ISBN 978-1-60699-779-6

Printed in China

GHOST of the GROTTO

FANTAGRAPHICS BOOKS

CONTENTS

ALL STORIES WRITTEN AND DRAWN BY CARL BARKS

WALT DISNEY
Donald Duck
and the
GHOST of the GROTTO
DONALD AND THE BOYS HAVE EMBARKED ON A NEW ADVENTURE. THEY HAVE RENTED A SMALL BOAT AND ARE GATHERING SEAWEED IN THE OCEAN WATERS AROUND THE ISLANDS OF THE WEST INDIES....

THIS SEAWEED BED IS ABOUT PLAYED OUT!
YES, UNCA' DONALD! IT'S TAKEN US ALL MORNING TO GATHER HALF A BOATLOAD!

IF WE'RE GOING TO MAKE ANY MONEY AT THIS KELP-GATHERING, WE'VE GOT TO FIND RICHER BEDS!

THERE IS LOTS OF KELP IN THE CENTER OF SKULL-EYE REEF— IF WE COULD ONLY GET TO IT!

YEAH, IF! NOBODY HAS EVER FIGURED A SAFE WAY TO GET THE KELP OUT OF THAT LAGOON, BUT WE'LL HAVE ANOTHER LOOK AT THE REEF ON OUR WAY BACK TO PORT!

THAT IS IT AHEAD—A DANGEROUS PLACE TO TAKE A BOAT!

WOW! WHAT KELP! HASN'T BEEN TOUCHED SINCE EVER!
MUST BE FATHOMS DEEP!
AND DOWN UNDER IT! I WONDER WHAT'S DOWN THERE!
CHINA, OL' SALT!

WE COULD DYNAMITE A CHANNEL THROUGH THE CORAL, BUT THAT WOULD COST MORE THAN THE IODINE FACTORY WOULD PAY US FOR THE KELP!

BACK TO PORT, BOYS! WE MAY AS WELL GIVE UP SKULL-EYE REEF AS A BAD DREAM!

NOT A VERY BIG LOAD TODAY, DONALD!
NOPE! THE KELP BEDS ARE PLAYING OUT!

TOUGH LUCK! THE PRICE OF KELP WENT UP ANOTHER DOLLAR A TON TODAY!
THE PRICE WENT UP **AGAIN**?

I'VE **GOT** TO FIGURE A WAY TO GET THE KELP OUT OF SKULL-EYE REEF!
TONIGHT IS THE NIGHT, FRANCHY!
OUI, M'SIEUR! TONIGHT EEZ ZE NIGHT!
GROG SHOP

CAN WE HELP YOU THINK, UNCA' DONALD?
YES! BY KEEPING QUIET!
TONIGHT BANE THE NIGHT, TONY!
EET EES SO! ALAS!

KEEP YOUR TYKES LOCKED UP TONIGHT, PEDRO!
SI, SI, SENOR! I KEEP THEEM EEN **SAFE** PLACE!

COME ON, KIDS! I CAN THINK OF ONLY ONE WAY TO GET THAT KELP! AND THAT IS THE **DANGEROUS** WAY!

THEY HAVE THE BOAT UNLOADED! WE'LL GO OUT TO SKULL-EYE REEF AND WAIT FOR THE TIDE! THE REST IS UP TO LUCK!

YE'RE NOT LEAVIN' THEM KIDS **UNGUARDED** TONIGHT, ARE YE, MATEY?
WHY NOT? HAVE THEY GOT **HYDROPHOBIA**?

BUT **TONIGHT**, MATEY! TONIGHT IS **THE** NIGHT!

THE NIGHT **WHAT**?
DON'T YE KNOW? TONIGHT **SOMEBODY'S LITTLE BOY WILL BE STOLEN!**

SOMEBODY'S KID, HUH? **WHO'S** GOIN' TO STEAL HIM?
NOBODY KNOWS!

WHY WILL HE BE STOLEN?
NOBODY KNOWS!

WELL, **WHY** WILL HE BE STOLEN **TONIGHT**?
NOBODY KNOWS!

GEE, YOU'RE FULL OF HELPFUL INFORMATION!
WAIT, SENOR! YOU ARE NEW TO THEES ISLAND! YOU HAF NOT HEARD OF EETS **MEESTERY**!

EVERY FEEFTY YEARS ON ZE NIGHT OF ZEES DATE A LEETLE BOY HAS BEEN STOLEN—AN' NEVER SEEN AGAIN!

ZAT HAS HAPPENED SEVEN TIMES EEN ZE CENTURIES SINCE ZE FIRST ONE DEESAPPEARED!
IT'S TIME YOU'RE DOING SOMETHING ABOUT IT!

WE ARE DOING SOME-THING! WE'RE LOCKING ALL OUR LEETLE BOYS EEN A SAFE PLACE TONIGHT!
WELL, I WON'T HAVE TO DO THAT! NO KIDNAPER WILL LOOK FOR BOYS ON SKULL-EYE REEF!

HASN'T THERE EVER BEEN ANY CLUE TO WHO DOES THE STEALING?
WELL, YES! THERE WAS ONE CLUE—LEFT A LONG TIME AGO! A FOOTPRINT!

A FOOTPRINT OF A MAN WEARING ARMOR!

A MAN IN ARMOR! DO YOU SUPPOSE THERE ARE KNIGHTS IN THESE INDIES?
PHOOEY! NOBODY HAS WORN ARMOR IN THESE ISLANDS SINCE THE DAYS OF THE GALLEONS!

SURE IS A MYSTERIOUS MYSTERY, IF YOU ASK ME!
GIVES ME DUCK PIMPLES!

LET THOSE ISLANDERS WORRY ABOUT THEIR MYSTERY! WE'VE GOT WORRIES OF OUR OWN – GETTING THIS BOAT ONTO SKULL-EYE REEF!

UNCA' DONALD, YOU **CAN'T** RUN THIS BOAT **ONTO** THE REEF! YOU'LL WRECK IT!
PHOOEY! I'LL SET IT DOWN ON THE CORAL AS GENTLY AS A FEATHER FALLS ...IF I'M **LUCKY**!

THERE'S THE REEF NOW, BUT YOU'D HARDLY KNOW IT! IT'S ALMOST UNDER WATER AT HIGH TIDE!

SOME OF THOSE LOW PLACES ARE DEEP ENOUGH TO BACK THE BOAT INTO— **MAYBE**!
I FEEL LUCKY! WE'LL TRY **THAT** ONE!

SNAGS AHEAD — I MEAN **ASTERN**!
DROP THE ANCHOR! THERE'S A BIG WAVE COMING!

HOLD, ANCHOR, HOLD! IF IT SLIPS, WE'LL GO OVER INTO THE LAGOON!

THUD!

WELL, I SET HER ON THE REEF, DIDN'T I?
YEAH! **GENTLY** AS A FEATHER FALLS!
THAT RATTLE YOU HEAR IS MY TEETH!

NOW TO LOAD HER WITH KELP AND FLOAT HER OFF AT HIGH TIDE TOMORROW!

HEAVE HO!
AND A MERRY YO HO!
FIFTEEN BARNACLES ON THE CAPTAIN'S CHEST!

THE TIDE EBBS!
MUST BE HOLES UNDER THE CORAL! THE LAGOON DRAINS AS THE OUTSIDE WATER GOES DOWN!

HEY! THROW THE TONGS INTO THAT BIG PILE OF KELP! MAYBE WE CAN YANK THE WHOLE MESS ABOARD!

LOOK! THERE'S SOMETHING UNDER THERE — AND IT'S NOT **CHINA**!

IT'S PART OF A **SHIP**! A WRECK THAT WAS WASHED OVER THE REEF!

I'LL YANK MORE KELP OFF THE THING! WE'LL SEE WHAT IT IS!

LATER!
IT'S AN OLD GALLEON!
OR A BRITISH MAN O' WAR! SEE THE GUN PORTS!

GET OUR RUBBER RAFT AND SOME LINES! WE'LL GO ABOARD AND HAVE A LOOK AT IT!

NOT MUCH LEFT TO TELL ITS HISTORY!

WATCH YOUR STEP, UNCA' DONALD! THAT DECK IS ROTTEN!

SPLASH!

GRAB THIS LINE, UNCA' DONALD! WE'LL PULL YOU OUT!

SQUEECH!

HELP!

YE CATS! IS ALL THAT ONE OCTOPUS?

WELL, THAT ENDS OUR EXPLORING!
PERIOD!

WE'LL COOK UP A SNACK OF VITTLES AND CRAWL INTO OUR BUNKS!

NIGHT!
I'VE GOT A CREEPY FEELING THAT ALL IS NOT WELL!
SAME HERE!
FINDING THAT OLD SHIP, AND HEARING ABOUT THAT ARMORED MAN IS TOO MUCH MYSTERY FOR ONE DAY!

SHUT UP AND GO TO SLEEP, OR YOU'LL FIND PINK STRIPES ON YOUR BACKS!

IF YOU KIDS BELIEVE THE WILD TALE THOSE ISLAND JERKS WERE BROADCASTING, YOU'RE CRAZIER THAN THEY ARE!

AND WHILE THE WEARY KELPERS SLEEP, THE MOON RIDES ONCE MORE ABOVE THE HULK OF THE ANCIENT MAN O'WAR!

CAN THAT BE THE CABIN DOOR SWINGING OPEN ON LONG-RUSTED HINGES?
CREAK!

TONIGHT IS YE NIGHT!

THE FIRST CRACK OF DAWN!
CRACK!
ROLL OUT, SAILORMEN! WE'VE GOT TO FINISH LOADING AND FLOAT OFF WHILE THE TIDE IS HIGH!

HUEY! START THE ENGINE!
LOUIE! OIL THE WINCHES!
AYE, AYE, SIR!
AYE, AYE, SIR!

DEWEY! STAND BY THE CAPSTAN AND KEEP THE ANCHOR CHAIN STRUMMING!
DEW-EEE!

WHERE IS THAT LAZY KID? **DEW-EEEEE!**

DEWEY!
HE ISN'T ON THE BOAT ANY PLACE, UNCA' DONALD!

HE WOULDN'T HAVE GONE FOR A WALK, BUT I'LL LOOK FOR HIS TRACKS, TO MAKE SURE!

WELL, WHAT ARE YOU SO GOGGLE-EYED ABOUT? DO YOU SEE TRACKS?

YES — THE TRACKS OF AN ARMORED MAN!

GREAT FISHES! THERE MAY BE SOMETHING IN THAT STORY, AFTER ALL!

WHERE COULD THE GUY HAVE GONE TO? HIS TRACKS HAVE BEEN WASHED OUT BY THE WAVES!

HE KIDNAPED DEWEY! THAT'S SURE! AND HE MUST HAVE TAKEN HIM TO THE ISLAND! THERE'S NO SIGN OF LIFE ON THIS REEF!

UNCA' DONALD! DO YOU SUPPOSE THAT ARMORED MAN COULD HAVE COME FROM THE OLD SHIP?

IF HE HAS HIS HIDE-OUT THERE, HE MUST HAVE GILLS LIKE A FISH! THE WHOLE SHIP IS UNDER WATER!
MAYBE HE'S
A GHOST!

GHOST, PHOOEY! HE **HAD** TO COME FROM THE ISLAND! WE'LL GO BACK TO PORT AND TEAR THE PLACE APART!

WE **CAN'T** GO BACK TO PORT, UNCA' DONALD!
WHADDA YA MEAN— **CAN'T**?

THERE'S A GREAT BIG HOLE IN OUR HULL THAT MIGHT HAVE BEEN CUT WITH A **SWORD**!

THE GUY DIDN'T WANT US TO GET TO THE POLICE! HE FIGURED US TO FLOAT THE BOAT OFF INTO DEEP WATER AND **SINK!**
YEAH! AND **ALL** DROWN!

HE SURE TAKES NO CHANCES ON GETTING CAUGHT!
NO WONDER HE'S BEEN ABLE TO PULL THESE JOBS FOR **FOUR HUNDRED YEARS** WITHOUT A SLIP-UP!

UNCA' DONALD, YOU DON'T THINK THE **SAME** GUY PULLED **ALL** THOSE KIDNAPINGS, DO YOU?
I DON'T KNOW WHAT TO THINK!

A GUY THAT RUNS AROUND IN TIN PANTS IN A HOT CLIMATE LIKE THIS IS CAPABLE OF ANYTHING!

WELL, WE CAN RADIO THE NEWS TO PORT, AND GET HELP OUT HERE! EVERY MINUTE COUNTS!

OF ALL THE DIRTY TRICKS! THAT IRON-PLATED CROOK STRIPPED THE WIRES OFF THE RADIO!

HE PROBABLY USED THEM TO TIE DEWEY! GET THE SIGNAL ROCKETS, HUEY!
AYE, AYE, SIR!

THE ROCKETS ARE NO GOOD ANY MORE, UNCA' DONALD! THEY WERE IN THE HOLD—AND THAT'S ALL FLOODED WITH WATER!

BOY! ARE WE EVER STUCK HERE! ARE WE EVER! BUT THERE'S ONE SLIM HOPE! GET SOME OIL WASTE AND LIGHT A SIGNAL FIRE! SOME PASSING SHIP MAY SEE IT!

THAT RIDGE IS THE HIGHEST POINT ON THE REEF! LIGHT THE FIRE THERE!

UNCA' DONALD! THERE'S A HOLE UP HERE!
COAST GUARD MAYBE HAD A FLAGPOLE THERE!

IT SOUNDS HOLLOW—LIKE THERE'S A BIG CAVERN UNDERNEATH!

A CAVERN UNDER THIS REEF WOULD JUST ABOUT TAKE THE CAKE!
I'LL YELL DOWN THE HOLE! YOU'LL HEAR IT ECHO!

HELLO! THIS IS **LOUIE!**

HELLO! THIS IS **DEWEY!**

DEWEY'S DOWN THERE!
CLONK!
HOW'D HE GET THERE?
LEMME LOOK!

THAT PUTS A WHOLE NEW FACE ON THE SITUATION! WE KNOW **WHERE** HE IS!
DEWEY, ARE YOU ALL RIGHT?

I'M IN — MMMF!
SOMEBODY CLAPPED A HAND OVER HIS MOUTH!
THE **ARMORED** MAN!

WE'LL BE RIGHT DOWN AND SAVE YOU, DEWEY! KEEP YOUR CHIN UP!

HOW ARE WE GONNA GET DOWN THERE, UNCA' DONALD? THAT HOLE ISN'T A SWINGING DOOR!
AND WE AREN'T GOPHERS!

THERE MUST BE AN **ENTRANCE** SOMEWHERE! SEARCH THE REEF! LOOK FOR HOLES ON EVERY POINT ABOVE THE TIDE LINE!

LATER!
THERE ISN'T ANOTHER HOLE IN THE WHOLE REEF, UNCA' DONALD!
THEN, WE'LL **MAKE** AN ENTRANCE OF **THIS** ONE!

GRAB THE TONGS, BOYS, AND HOOK 'EM INTO THE CORAL! WE'LL YANK THE WHOLE ROOF OFF THAT KIDNAPER'S FOXHOLE!
WHIRR!

AND IF YOU CAN GET THE TONGS INTO OLD TIN PANTS, WE'LL YANK **HIM** OUT OF THERE, TOO!
RIP!

THAT AFTER-NOON!
OKAY, UNCA' DONALD!
THERE'S ROOM NOW TO GET THROUGH THE HOLE!
SWELL! STAND BY TO LOWER ME DOWN!

YOU'RE NOT GOING INTO THAT CAVERN EMPTY-HANDED, ARE YOU, UNCA' DONALD?

NO! I'M TAKING THIS TWELVE-GAUGE **CAN OPENER**, SO I CAN MAKE A DENT IN THAT TIN OF MEDIEVAL SAUSAGE!

YOU'RE TAKING AN AWFUL CHANCE, UNCA' DONALD!
THERE MAY BE A WHOLE **SWARM** OF ARMORED MEN DOWN THERE!
I DON'T CARE IF THERE'S A FOUNDRY FULL OF SHERMAN TANKS — **I'M GOING DOWN**!

LOWER ME, BOYS!

HOIST ME, BOYS!

YOU'VE LOST YOUR SHOTGUN, UNCA' DONALD!
WHAT'LL WE DO NOW?
WELL, WE'RE NOT GIVING UP! THAT'S A CINCH!

WE FORGOT TO LIGHT OUR SIGNAL FIRE! GET IT GOING!
AYE, AYE, SIR!

SWISH!
HEY! HE'S PUTTING OUR FIRE OUT!

THAT'S NOT FAIR! COME OUT OF YOUR HOLE AND FIGHT, YOU CAST-IRON GOPHER!
TAKE IT EASY, UNCA' DONALD! LISTEN TO US!

WE'VE GOT THAT GUY **BOTHERED**!
YEAH! HE'S SCARED WE'LL GET HELP OUT HERE!
SO WHAT?

DON'T YOU SEE? BEFORE HE LETS US GET A SIGNAL FIRE GOING, HE'LL COME OUT OF HIS CAVE AND TRY TO PUT IT OUT!
WE'LL BUILD THE NEXT FIRE FARTHER AWAY AND LURE HIM INTO THE OPEN!

THAT'S AN **IDEA**, KIDS! WE'LL LIGHT THE FIRE NEAR OUR BOAT, SO WE CAN USE THE TONGS ON HIM IF HE COMES CLOSE!

THE TIDE'S OUT AGAIN!
YEAH, AND THAT OLD SHIP IS SHOWING AGAIN! IT GIVES ME THE CREEPS!

NIGHT!
IT'S DARK NOW! HE'LL BE SURE TO COME OUT OF HIS HOLE!

KEEP WATCHING THE TOP OF THE REEF! THAT'S WHERE HE'LL FIRST APPEAR!
YEAH! WE'LL BE ABLE TO SEE HIM AGAINST THE GLOW OF THE WATER!

ABOARD THE OLD SHIP!
YON VARLETS BODE ILL! THEY MUST BE SLAIN, AND THEIR ACCURSED FIRE THROWN INTO YE SEA!

UNCA' DONALD, I'M SURE THERE'S SOMETHING MOVING ON THAT OLD SHIP! I HEARD A DOOR CREAK JUST NOW!
PROBABLY THE OCTOPUS FEELING AROUND!

THE STERN OF THE OLD SHIP SWINGS OPEN!
WITH MY TRUSTY BLADE I MUST SALLY FORTH!

BONNIE QUEEN BESS WILL KNIGHT ME FOR THIS NIGHT'S WORK!

DON'T YOU THINK ONE OF US SHOULD WATCH THE REEF BEHIND US?
NO! HE'LL COME FROM THAT SIDE OF THE FIRE!

WE'LL SEE HIM BEFORE HE SEES US! DON'T WORRY!

I'M GETTING HUNGRY! HAND ME ONE OF THOSE TOMATOES FROM OUR LUNCH BASKET!

PHOOEY! THAT ONE WAS OVERRIPE!

ODDS BODKINS!
SPLOK!

THE ARMORED MAN!
A RASH ON YE, VARLETS!

SWISH

SCATTER, KIDS! HIDE IN THE KELP!
SLASH!

THEY HAVE ESCAPED MY BLADE! AN THOUSAND PLAGUES BESET THEM!

HOWBEIT, THEIR ACCURSED FIRE SHALL NOT BURN THIS NIGHT!

HE KICKED OUR FIRE INTO THE SEA AND DISAPPEARED!
HE'S AROUND SOME PLACE LOOKING FOR US!

I DON'T SEE HIM NEAR THE BOAT! LET'S SNEAK BACK AND SNAP THE SEARCHLIGHT ON!

YOU WORK THE LIGHT, LOUIE, AND I'LL STAND BY TO SWING THE TONGS ON HIM THE INSTANT WE SPOT HIM!

HE'S GONE! HE'S NOT ON THE REEF **ANY PLACE**!

WONDER WHY HE WENT BACK TO HIS HOLE BEFORE HE'D HUNTED US DOWN?
HE WAS IN AN AWFUL HURRY FOR SOME REASON!

LISTEN! THERE'S THAT CREAKIN' SOUND AGAIN! IT COMES FROM THE OLD SHIP!

TURN THE LIGHT THAT WAY! WE'LL SEE WHAT'S MAKIN' OVER THERE!

THE ARMORED MAN IS GOING INTO A HOLE IN THE STERN!

I'LL BE DOGGONED! **THAT'S** WHERE THE CAVE ENTRANCE IS! UNDER THAT OLD SHIP!
SNAP!

BUT, UNCA' DONALD! HOW CAN HE GO IN AND OUT THROUGH THE SHIP? WHY DOESN'T THE OCTOPUS EAT HIM?

WELL, I SUPPOSE THAT EVEN AN OCTOPUS KNOWS WHAT IT CAN **DIGEST**!

ANYWAY, WE KNOW WHY THE GUY SCOOTED BACK TO HIS CAVE SO FAST! HE HAD TO GET THROUGH THE ENTRANCE BEFORE THE TIDE COVERED IT!
YEAH! SINCE IT'S **UNDER** THE OLD SHIP, IT MUST BE UNDER WATER MOST OF THE TIME!

YOU SURE MADE YOURSELF A MESS OF TROUBLE WHEN YOU KIDNAPED ME, HUH, JINGLE JOINTS?
VERILY, THEE SAYETH A BOOKFUL!

LIGHT ANOTHER SIGNAL FIRE! WE'LL WAIT FOR THE NEXT LOW TIDE, AND, IF HELP HASN'T COME, WE'LL STORM THAT GUY'S FRONT DOOR WITH EVERYTHING WE'VE GOT!

AND IN THE MEANTIME WE'VE GOT TO THINK OF A WAY TO GET PAST THAT OCTOPUS!
OR GET RID OF HIM ALTOGETHER!

LOW TIDE NEXT DAY!
WHAT ARE YOU DOING WITH THAT CHUNK OF MEAT, HUEY?
I'M ROLLING IT FULL OF **CHILI PEPPER**! I'VE FIGURED A WAY TO GET RID OF THE OCTOPUS!

AFTER HE SWALLOWS THIS HE'LL BE TOO BUSY HOLDING HIS STOMACH TO MAKE ANY PASSES AT US!

SOUNDS LIKE A CORNY IDEA, BUT I'LL SWING THE MEAT OVER WITH THE TONGS AND DROP IT DOWN THE HATCH!

SWISH

SMACK!
CHOMP! CHOMP!
HE'S EATING IT, UNCA' DONALD! HEAR HIM?
GULP!

UH OH! I MUSTA USED A SPRINKLE TOO MUCH PEPPER!

HE'S GONE CRAZY!
GONE—PERIOD!
WONDER WHAT HE'D GIVE FOR A TON OF ICE CREAM!

WE'RE RID OF THE OLD SHIP AND THE OCTOPUS, TOO! WHAT A BREAK!
NOW WE CAN SEE THE CAVE ENTRANCE!

IT'S A HIGH POINT OF CORAL, AND THERE'S A WATERTIGHT LID ON IT!
MAYBE LOCKED FROM BELOW!

IT WON'T BE HARD TO OPEN WITH THE TONGS! BUT THEN WHAT?
I HAVE A PLAN! ALL I NEED IS A SQUIRT GUN AND A COUPLE OF MICE!

MICE!
YES! GO SEE IF THERE ARE ANY IN THE TRAPS WE HAVE SET IN THE GALLEY!

THERE WAS ONLY **ONE**, UNCA' DONALD!
HE'LL DO! I LIKE THE GLINT IN HIS EYES!
GRR!

NOW FILL THIS SQUIRT GUN WITH ROACH POWDER, AND I'LL BE OFF TO THE WARS!
SNARL!

GOING TO BATTLE AN ARMORED MAN WITH A SQUIRT GUN AND A MOUSE! DO YOU SUPPOSE UNCA' DONALD'S IN HIS RIGHT MIND?
I HOPE NOT! HIS SENSIBLE IDEAS **NEVER** WORK!
GRR!

OKAY, BOYS! SWING THE TONGS OVER HERE!

WHEN I GIVE THE SIGNAL, HEAVE HO!

READY—GO!

UH, OH! I EXPECTED YOU TO POP UP WITH A **SWORD**!

DONALD DUCKS IN THE NICK OF TIME!
BOOM!

PWOOF!

BONK!
CLANK!
CLATTER!
CRASH

COME ON, MONT-MORENCY, WE'RE GOIN' DOWN!
SNARL!

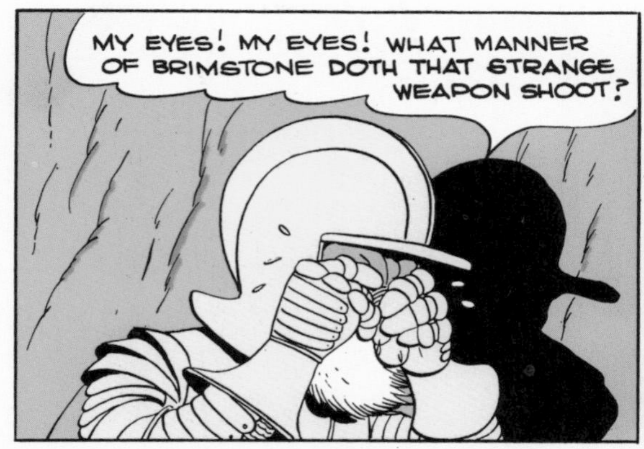
MY EYES! MY EYES! WHAT MANNER OF BRIMSTONE DOTH THAT STRANGE WEAPON SHOOT?

IN YOU GO, MONTMORENCY! IT'S **YOUR** JOB TO GET OUT!
GRR!

YEEOWCH! I'M **ASSAILED** FROM ALL QUARTERS!

A **DEMON** IS LOOSE IN MY ARMOR!
BOING!

I CAN'T STAND IT!
CLANG!
CLANK!

TAKE IT OFF! TAKE IT OFF! TAKE IT OFF!

THAT'S BETTER!
CLANK!
BONG!

NOW WE FACE EACH OTHER ON EVEN TERMS, SIR BOILER SHIRT!
SNARL!

COUNT **US** IN, UNCA' DONALD!
WE CAME DOWN THE OTHER ENTRANCE AND RESCUED DEWEY!
HERE I AM! YIPPEE!

I **SURRENDER!** WHAT WILL MY LORD, SIR FRANCIS DRAKE, THINK OF ME?

I HAVE **FAILED** IN MY TRUST! YE GOLD OF HER GRACIOUS MAJESTY WAS NOT SAFE IN MY KEEPING!
GOLD?

PILLAGE, AS THEE MUST KNOW, FROM AN DOZEN GALLEONS OF OUR SPANISH ENEMIES!

WOW! THE PLOT THICKENS! WHAT'S THE LOWDOWN ON ALL THIS—I MEAN, WHAT IS **YE** STORY?

I SEE NO HARM IN ITS TELLING, LADS! MY LORD, SIR FRANCIS, WILL HAVE ME HANGED, ANYWAY!
HAVE
YOU
HANGED?

ODDS BODKINS! THIS GUY THINKS SIR FRANCIS DRAKE IS **STILL ALIVE!**

IT IS A STRANGE STORY THEY WRING FROM THE MYSTERIOUS OLD MAN!
LONG AGO, YE OLD SHIP UP YONDER WAS BOUND FOR ENGLAND, BEARING THIS GOLD TO YE COFFERS OF GOOD QUEEN BESS —
AND THE SHIP WAS WASHED OVER THIS REEF IN A GREAT STORM, I BET!

AYE, LAD! AND THERE WAS BUT ONE SURVIVOR!
YOU?

NO! YE CAPTAIN! HE, IN WHOSE TRUST WAS YE KEEPING OF YE TREASURE!
THANKS! NOW I CAN START BELIEVING YE CALENDAR AGAIN!

AND THAT HE SAVED YE GOLD WAS DUE TO A STROKE OF GREAT FORTUNE!

WHEN YE SHIP CRASHED OVER YE REEF IT BURST YON HOLE IN YE ROOF OF THIS GREAT GROTTO!
AND HE LUGGED THE STUFF DOWN HERE?

AYE! AND SUCH STORES AS WOULD SERVE HIM UNTIL YE COMING OF SIR FRANCIS! HE KNEW NOT HOW **LONG** — HOW **VERY** LONG THAT WOULD BE!

THE YEARS SPED, AND MY CAPTAIN GREW **OLD**! LEST HE DIE AND LEAVE THE GOLD UNTENDED, HE TOOK HIS SMALL BOAT ONE NIGHT AND SALLIED FORTH!

FROM YE ISLAND OFF YONDER HE STOLE A SMALL BOY TO BE GUARDIAN OF YE GOLD AFTER HIS PASSING!
YE MYSTERY IS UNRAVELING! GO ON!

HE WAS REARED TO THINK AS YE CAPTAIN THOUGHT, AND TO GUARD YE GOLD WITH HIS LIFE! BUT HE, TOO, GREW **OLD**!
AND HE, TOO, STOLE A BOY! THE SECRET OF THOSE KIDNAPINGS IS OUT!

ON EACH PASSING OF YE HALF CENTURY, YE GUARD HAS BEEN RENEWED!
THEN IT CAME **YOUR** TURN TO PULL THE JOB!

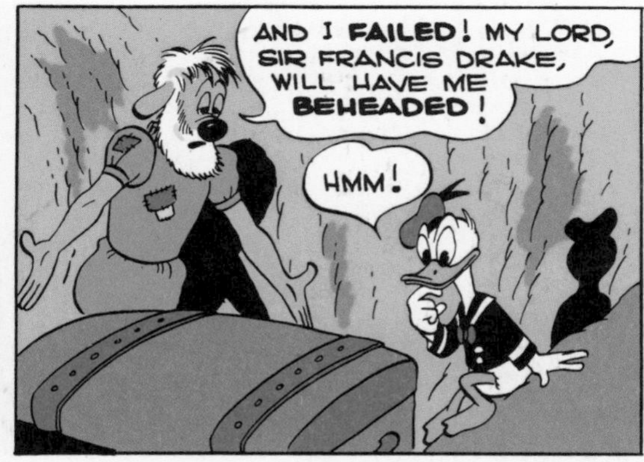
AND I **FAILED!** MY LORD, SIR FRANCIS DRAKE, WILL HAVE ME **BEHEADED**!
HMM!

HOW DO YOU KNOW **I'M** NOT SIR FRANCIS DRAKE, COME TO CLAIM YE QUEEN'S LONG-LOST VALUABLES?
I **KNOW**!

IN THIS OLD BOOK IS A **PICTURE** OF SIR FRANCIS— AND **YE BE NOT HE!**..NYAAH!

NO SOAP, UNCA' DONALD! YOU'LL NOT GET THE GOLD WITH A SOUR GAG LIKE THAT ONE!
GRR!

NEXT DAY THE SIGNAL FIRE BRINGS RESCUE— AND FAME! FOR ON THE ISLAND THE DUCKS ARE HEROES, THAT IS!
HERE IS THE KEY TO THE CITY! ANY FAVOR YOU ASK WILL BE GRANTED!
THEN, HOW ABOUT ME GETTING THAT GOLD WE FOUND IN THE CAVE?

SORRY, MISTER DUCK, BUT THE LAW SAYS THAT GOLD BELONGS TO THE MAN THAT WAS GUARDING IT!
A RASH ON YE WHOLE BUSINESS!
MAYOR

AND THE ARMORED MAN— HOW IS HE TAKING THIS SUDDEN TURN OF EVENTS?
ANOTHER OF YE HAMBURGERS, SCULLERY KNAVE! THEY TASTE MIGHTYE GOODE AFTER AN HALF CENTURY OF YE FISH!
TONY'S BURGER PALACE
YE END

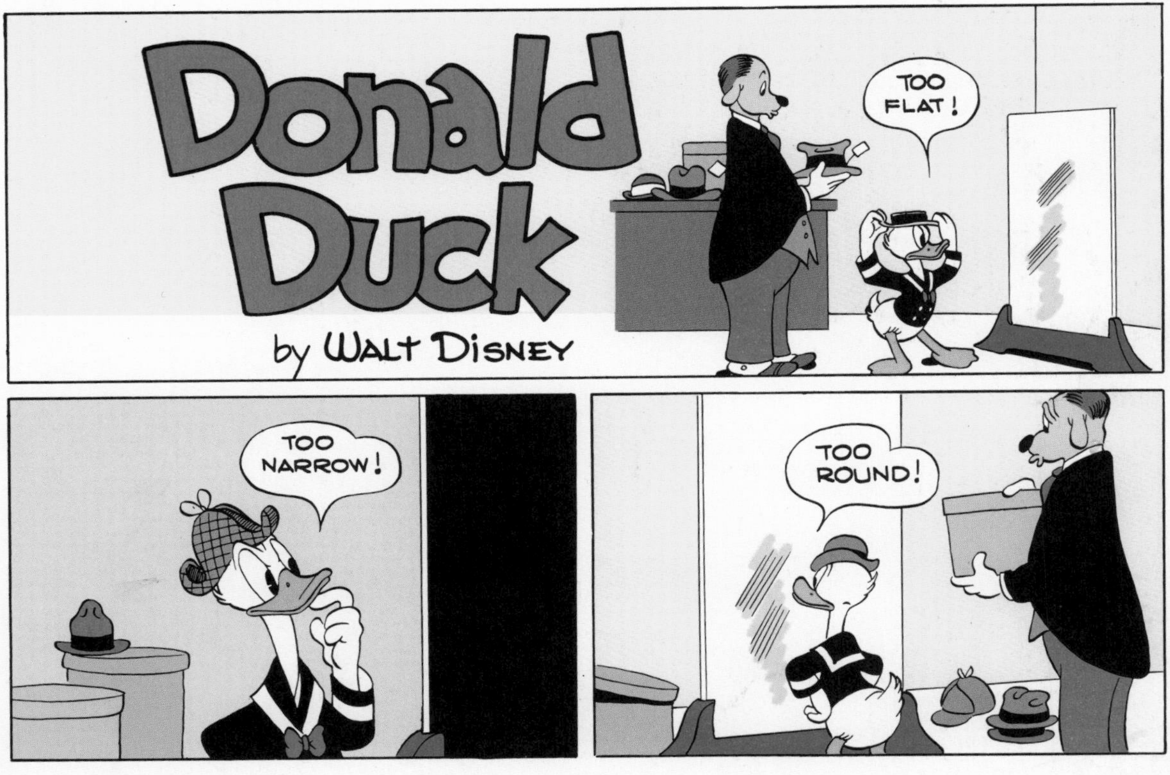

Donald Duck

by WALT DISNEY

TOO FLAT!

THE END

Donald Duck

By Walt Disney

THOSE BIG VISORS ARE REALLY CLASSY!

AHHHHHHHH!

I'LL TROMP HER UP TO FIFTY AND ROAR PAST DAISY'S HOUSE!

HEY! THE CAR'S LEAVING THE GROUND!

WELL?

THE END

WALT DISNEY presents

DONALD DUCK

"MAYOR PLANS CONTEST FOR FLOWER GROWERS!"

DAILY GRUMBLE

I CAN SEE THIS BACKYARD BLOOMING WITH COLORFUL POSIES! BEDS OF POPPYHOCKS, LILIES OF THE DALE! SPRIGS OF EVENING GLORIES! I KNOW ALL ABOUT FLOWERS!
STICK YOUR BEAK OUTA THAT FOXHOLE AND YOU'LL GET A BOMB ON THE BEAN!
KEEP YOUR OWN NECK IN, OR I'LL BEND IT WITH A V-2!
TANK

BUT,
UNCA'
DONALD!
GET OUT!

AND AFTER WE WORKED
A WHOLE WEEK
DIGGING THOSE FOXHOLES!
TANK

WHERE ARE WE GONNA PLAY, UNCA' DONALD?
WE CAN'T PLAY IN THE STREET!

YOU DON'T NEED TO PLAY! YOU CAN GO IN THE HOUSE AND READ BOOKS! IT'LL BE BETTER FOR YOU!

HERE'S A BOOK ON "REMOVING MUSTY SMELLS FROM DRIED DODO FEATHERS"! READ IT AND IMPROVE YOUR MINDS!

MUTINY!

SNAPPING DRAGONS AND JOHNNY-HOP-UPS WILL LOOK BEST ALONGSIDE THE SWEET-EYED SUSANS!

THERE, IT'S ALL LEVELED! NOW TO PLANT THE SEEDS AND WAIT FOR THE PRIZE MONEY!

LATER!
UNCA' DONALD IS THROUGH SEEDING! WHEN HE LEAVES WE'LL GO OUTSIDE AND PLAY AGAIN!

I'LL REST AWHILE, THEN GO DOWN-TOWN AND ENTER MY NAME IN THE CONTEST!

WE CAN RUN RACES BETWEEN THE ROWS!
YEAH! AND PLAY HOPSCOTCH AMONG THE FLOWER BEDS!

GET BACK TO YOUR BOOK! IF I CATCH YOU IN MY GARDEN AGAIN, I'LL BOIL YOU IN VINEGAR!

THIS IS AWFUL! WE'LL GROW UP TO BE SICKLY AND WEAK!
YEAH! HEALTHY KIDS NEED LOTS OF FRESH AIR AND SUNSHINE!
AND LOTS OF **PLAY**!
WE **READ** EVERY DAY IN SCHOOL!

I'M SURE THE KIDS WILL STAY IN THE HOUSE NOW! I GAVE 'EM A GOOD SCARE!

I'LL GO DOWNTOWN AND SIGN UP FOR THE CONTEST!

I MADE IT ACROSS THE GARDEN IN FOUR SKIPS AND THREE HOPS!
I DIDN'T! I LANDED IN UNCA' DONALD'S PANSY BED!

LATER!
GREAT SUFFERIN' SUNFLOWERS! THOSE KIDS ARE IN MY GARDEN AGAIN!

I'LL WHIP THE FEATHERS OFF OF YOU!

"MUSTINESS IS CAUSED BY KEEPING THINGS INDOORS OUT OF THE SUNLIGHT!"
LIKE US!
WE'LL GET MUSTY!

I HAVE TO FIGURE A WAY TO KEEP THE KIDS OUT OF MY GARDEN! THEY'LL BE OUT THERE EVERY TIME MY BACK IS TURNED!

I COULD PUT **TACKS** ON THE GROUND...BUT THAT'D KEEP **ME** OUT, **TOO**!
OH, OH! THERE'S SOMEBODY AT THE DOOR!
KNOCK! KNOCK!

SAY, MISTER! WOULD YOU LIKE TO BUY A HIVE OF BEES?
BEES? WHAT IN BLAZES WOULD I WANT WITH BEES? SCRAM!

BEES!

HEY! WAIT A MINUTE, MISTER! SURE, I'LL BUY YOUR BEES!

NEXT DAY!
UNCA' DONALD MUST BE AWAY!
I DON'T SEE HIM AROUND!

LET'S HAVE ANOTHER FOOTRACE THROUGH THE GARDEN!
YIPPEE!

WHAT'S THAT FUNNY BOX UNCA' DONALD HAS PUT IN THE GARDEN?
BUZZZ

THERE'S SOMETHING IN IT THAT KEEPS BUZZING!
BUZZ

BEES!

OW!

PUTTING THAT BEEHIVE OUT THERE WAS A DIRTY TRICK!
HOW ARE WE GONNA PLAY?

IF WE CAN GET A ROPE AROUND THE HIVE, WE CAN DRAG IT DOWN THE STREET!

GRAB THE ROPE AND START PULLING!

HEAVE HO!

UH, OH! WE ONLY PULLED THE THING APART!
BZZZZ

WOW! ARE THOSE BEES EVER MAD!

RUN FOR YOUR LIVES! OW!
OUCH!

HEH! HEH! HEH! THAT WILL BE THE LAST TIME THE KIDS TRY TO PLAY IN MY GARDEN!

I'LL SET THE HIVE BACK UP AGAIN! LUCKY I'M ONE OF THOSE PERSONS THAT BEES WON'T STING!

CAN YOU BEAT THAT?
BEES WON'T STING HIM!
WELL, AFTER ALL, A BEE MUST DRAW THE LINE SOMEWHERE!

WE MAY AS WELL GET BACK TO OUR BOOK!
WAIT! DON'T GIVE UP WITHOUT A FIGHT!

IF THE BEES WOULD **STING** UNCA' DONALD, HE'D GET **RID** OF THEM!
YEAH, BUT THEY DON'T LIKE THE WAY HE SMELLS, OR SOMETHIN'!

IT'S THAT STRONG SOAP HE USES! WE'LL HAVE TO FIX HIM SO THAT THE BEES **CAN'T LEAVE HIM ALONE**!

ATTAR OF ROSES, ESSENCE OF LILACS, EAU DE HONEYSUCKLE! THIS MIXTURE WILL DRIVE BEES MAD! BRING ME A SPRAY GUN, BOYS!

LUCKY UNCA' DONALD IS TAKING A NAP!

LATER!
HO HUM! GUESS I'LL GO OUT AND SEE HOW THE GARDEN GROWS!

HEY. WHAT'S GOIN' ON? BEES NEVER CAME THIS CLOSE TO ME **BEFORE**!

SCRAM, YOU HAGGLIN' HORNETS!
OW! THEY'RE **STINGING** ME!

I MUST BEAT 'EM TO THE DOOR, OR I'M A GONER!

SAFE! NOT A BEE GOT IN!
SLAM!

WAK! THEY'RE COMING THROUGH THE KEYHOLE!

I'LL PLUG IT WITH MY THUMB TILL I SPOT SOMETHING TO STOP IT UP!

OW!

NO MORE WRANGLING WASPS WILL GET IN **THIS** HOUSE!

NOW SHALL WE OPEN THE WINDOWS?
YES! IT'S GETTING STUFFY IN HERE!

HELP!
I'M SURROUNDED!

THEY'RE ALL OVER THE HOUSE! THE ATTIC IS MY ONLY HOPE!

I CAN HIDE IN THIS TRUNK TILL THEY GO AWAY!

NOW SHALL WE MAKE A DEAL WITH UNCA' DONALD?
THERE'S PLENTY OF TIME! LET'S GO PLAY IN THE YARD!
BUZZ!

HOURS LATER!
I CAN'T STAND THIS MUCH LONGER! I'M HOT AND THIRSTY!
BUZZ!

HELP, HUEY, LOUIE, AND DEWEY!

GET SOME RAGS AND SMOKE THESE BEES AWAY FROM HERE!
THAT'S AN AWFUL BIG JOB, UNCA' DONALD!

WE'RE **WEAK** FROM DOIN' SO MUCH **READING**!
YEAH! OUR MUSCLES ARE TOO FLABBY
TO LIFT A CLOUD OF SMOKE!

QUIT STALLING AND GET BUSY!
WELL, **MAYBE**... IF WE CAN MAKE A **DEAL** WITH YOU!
YEAH! WE WANT TO TALK **BUSINESS**!

OKAY! OKAY! I'LL AGREE TO ANYTHING YOU SAY! BUT GET THESE BEES AWAY FROM HERE BEFORE I SUFFOCATE!

AND SO ANOTHER DAY DAWNS OVER THE BACKYARD FENCE!
I MIGHT HAVE KNOWN I COULD NEVER RAISE FLOWERS WITH THOSE KIDS AROUND!
BUZZ!

UNCA' DONALD HAS THIS PART OF THE YARD SO LEVEL IT'S PERFECT FOR PLAYING BALL!
BATTER UP!

MISTER DUCK, AS MAYOR OF THIS FAIR CITY, I TAKE GREAT PLEASURE IN PRESENTING YOU WITH THIS FIRST PRIZE —
$

BUT I HAVEN'T ANY **FLOWER GARDEN**, YOUR HONOR! I'M NOT EVEN IN THE CONTEST ANY MORE!

THE PRIZE ISN'T FOR FLOWER GARDENS, MR. DUCK! IT'S FOR HAVING THE **HEALTHIEST BOYS IN TOWN**!
$

NOW WHAT DO YOU SUPPOSE HAS COME OVER UNCA' DONALD?
I CAN'T FIGURE HIM OUT! HE'S **MAD** ONE MINUTE AND **WHISTLING** THE NEXT!
BATTER UP!

THE END

DONALD DUCK

BY WALT DISNEY

I'M LOOKING FOR DONALD DUCK! CAN YOU TELL ME HOW I CAN FIND HIM, MISTER?

HMM! I'LL HAVE SOME FUN WITH THIS GUY!

INSURANCE

HEY, YOU! I FOLLOWED YOUR DIRECTIONS AND CAME OUT BACK HERE AGAIN! WHAT'S THE OTHER WAY TO FIND DONALD DUCK?

WAL, STRANGER, THE OTHER WAY IS TO SHAKE MY HAND AND SAY, "HELLO, DONALD!"

I'M HIM!

I GUESS THAT WASN'T SUCH A GOOD JOKE, AFTER ALL!

THE END

DONALD DUCK

By WALT DISNEY

I MUST TRY OUT MY NEW MODERN KITCHEN!

THE END

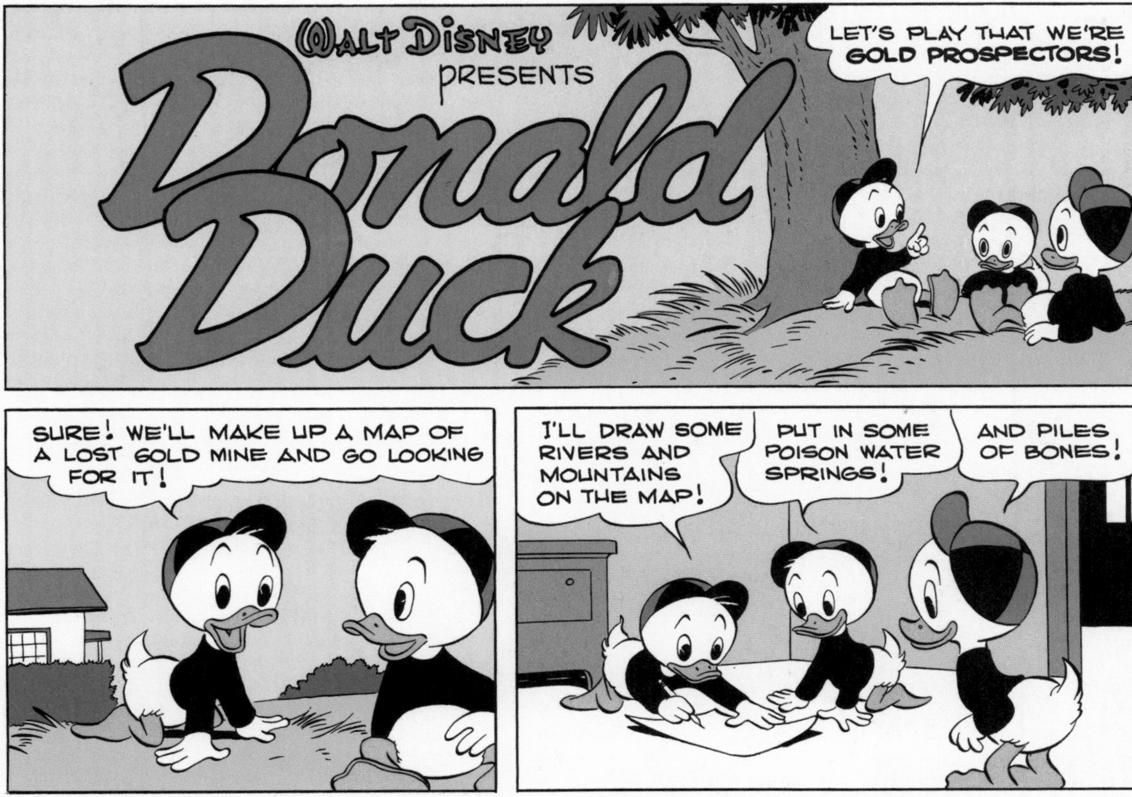

WALT DISNEY PRESENTS

Donald Duck

LET'S PLAY THAT WE'RE **GOLD PROSPECTORS!**

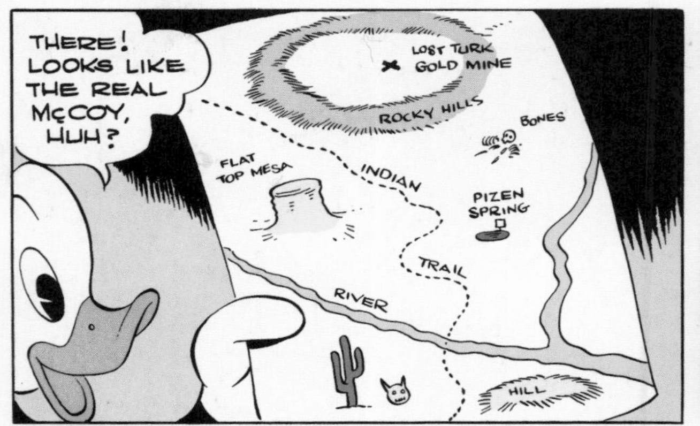
THERE! LOOKS LIKE THE REAL McCOY, HUH?
LOST TURK GOLD MINE
ROCKY HILLS
BONES
FLAT TOP MESA
INDIAN
PIZEN SPRING
TRAIL
RIVER
HILL

NOW LET'S GO SEE WHAT IT WILL LEAD US TO!
WE'LL PRETEND THAT MUD CREEK IS THE RIVER IN THE MAP!

THE MAP SHOWS A TRAIL GOING TOWARD THE HILLS! WE'LL PRETEND THIS COWPATH IS THE TRAIL!

WAIT A MINUTE! I JUST SAW A **FISH** IN THIS POOL! PHOOEY ON FINDING GOLD MINES! LET'S GO **FISHING**!

YOU DID SEE A FISH!
THROW THAT MAP AWAY AND RUN HOME FOR OUR POLES, WHILE I KEEP AN EYE ON HIM!

SO AWAY GOES THE MAP OF THE "LOST TURK GOLD MINE," SAILING DOWN THE WIND!

IT COMES TO REST ON A PILE OF ASHES AT THE CITY DUMP!

I'LL GO DOWN TO THE CITY DUMP AND SEE IF I CAN FIND A SPARE HEADLIGHT FOR MY CAR!

WELL, WELL! A PIECE OF PAPER! LOOKS LIKE A MAP!

IT IS A MAP— OF A LOST GOLD MINE!

SOMETIMES THESE THINGS LEAD TO A FORTUNE! I'LL TAKE THIS RIGHT HOME AND CHECK IT!

THERE'S A CACTUS ON THE MAP, SO THE MINE MUST BE SOMEWHERE IN THE SOUTHWEST!
DRAKE'S ATLAS

HERE IT IS! A SPOT IN NEW MEXICO WHERE A RIVER FORKS, AND A FLAT-TOPPED MESA STANDS NEAR SOME ROCKY HILLS!

THAT'S ALL I NEED TO KNOW! NEW MEXICO, HERE I COME!

GEE! UNCA' DONALD IS LOADING VALISES IN THE CAR! WONDER WHAT'S UP!

PACK SOME EXTRA CLOTHES IN A BAG, KIDS, AND PILE IN! WE'RE GOIN' TO NEW MEXICO!
!
!

TO **NEW MEXICO**!
WHY, UNCA' DONALD?
NEVER MIND **WHY**!

IF I TOLD YOU, YOU'D LET THE **SECRET** OUT, AND THERE'D BE TEN THOUSAND GUNMEN FOLLOWING US TO SEE WHERE I GO!

UNCA' DONALD MUST BE ON THE TRAIL OF SOMETHING **IMPORTANT**!
YEAH! **AWFUL** IMPORTANT!

TAKE IT EASY, UNCA' DONALD! NEW MEXICO WILL STAY WHERE IT IS TILL YOU GET THERE!
US
66

MILES AND MILES LATER!
THANK GOODNESS, WE'RE HERE!
DON'T RELAX YET, BOYS! THE WORST PART OF THE JOURNEY IS STILL AHEAD!
NEW MEXICO STATE LINE

LET'S SEE THIS ROAD MAP! I TURN NORTH ABOUT TWENTY MILES BEYOND THE NEXT TOWN!

GAS HER UP, AND SELL ME SOME SAND LUGS FOR MY TIRES — AND DON'T ASK ANY QUESTIONS!
313

ALONG HERE SOME PLACE IS THE TRAIL WHERE I TURN OFF!

YEP! THERE IT IS! GOES DOWN TOWARD THE FORK OF THAT DRY RIVER! PUT ON THE SAND LUGS, BOYS!
SQUEECH!

THIS IS THE RIVER CROSSING, ALL RIGHT! JUST WHERE IT SAYS ON THE MA—... ..I MEAN, JUST WHERE IT SHOULD BE!

HOW DOES UNCA' DONALD **KNOW** SO MUCH ABOUT THIS COUNTRY?
SEARCH ME! HE MUSTA BEEN TALKIN' TO THE JACK RABBITS!

UNCA' DONALD —
SIT STILL AND DON'T ASK QUESTIONS!
HOW **CAN** WE SIT STILL WHEN THERE IS NOTHING **UNDER** US HALF THE TIME?

THERE'S THE FLAT-TOPPED MESA! DOESN'T LOOK JUST LIKE THE ONE ON THE MAP, BUT THOSE OLD PROSPECTORS COULDN'T DRAW VERY GOOD!

THE MINE SHOULD BE JUST OVER THAT LOW PASS — IN THAT RING OF HILLS!

WHOA! THIS IS WHERE I GET OUT, BOYS!
THANK GOODNESS!

YOU KIDS STAY HERE, IN THE CAR! I'LL BE BACK IN A COUPLE OF HOURS WITH SOMETHING THAT'LL MAKE YOUR EYES POP!

AND IF YOU SEE ANYBODY COMING, GET THAT **OLD MAP** OUT OF MY GRIP AND BURY IT UNDER A ROCK!

NO DOUBT I'M THE **ONLY** GUY THAT KNOWS ABOUT THIS OLD MINE, BUT I'LL KEEP MY EYES AND EARS OPEN, ANYWAY!

THE TOP OF THE PASS—AND **ALL'S WELL**!

GO BACK, BUD! THIS IS JUST A **WARNING**!
POW!

THAT MUST BE ANOTHER GOLD HUNTER! WELL, IF HE THINKS HE CAN STOP **ME**—!

I'LL GET AROUND BEHIND HIM AND STOP **HIM**!

I HEAR HIM GOING DOWN TOWARD WHERE HE SAW ME LAST!

THERE'S HIS SHADOW ON THE ROCKS! HE'S RIGHT BELOW ME!

AN EYE FOR AN EYE, BUD!

THAT TAKES CARE OF HIM!
OW!

NOW OVER THE PASS TO THE LOST TURK GOLD MINE!

WHAT IN THUNDERATION? ??
KILROY WAS HERE!
THIS IS IT!

THE WHOLE VALLEY HAS BEEN PAINTED TO LOOK LIKE A **TARGET**! AND THE BULL'S-EYE IS RIGHT WHERE THE **MINE** SHOULD BE!

THIS IS IT!
IF SOMEBODY'S BEEN **KIDDING** DONALD DUCK, THERE'LL BE SOME BUSTED NOSES AROUND HERE!

I'LL GO RIGHT OUT THERE AND TAKE POSSESSION OF THE MINE! THEN LET ANYBODY **TRY** TO THROW ME OUT!

UNCA' DONALD SURE IS MYSTERIOUS ABOUT THIS BUSINESS!
YEAH! I WONDER WHAT THAT MAP IS THAT HE WANTED US TO BURY!

IT'S IN HIS VALISE! LET'S TAKE A LOOK BEFORE HE GETS BACK!

IT'S — WELL, I'LL BE A BOW-LEGGED MONGOOSE!

IT'S THAT CRAZY MAP **WE** DREW THE OTHER DAY!
BUT UNCA' DONALD WOULDN'T FOLLOW A GOOFY THING LIKE **THAT**!

BUT HE **HAS**! LOOK! THERE'S THE FLAT-TOP MESA, AND HERE ARE THE ROCKY HILLS!
WE'VE GOT TO **STOP** UNCA' DONALD BEFORE HE GOES ANY FARTHER!

HE WENT THROUGH THAT LOW PASS!

UNCA' DONALD!
COME
BACK!

GROAN!

GROAN!
THAT MUST BE UNCA' DONALD GROANING!
HE'S FALLEN AND HURT HISSELF!

WAK! IT'S A SOLDIER!

DID YOU SEE OUR UNCLE PASS THIS WAY?
HE'S A LITTLE GUY!
DID I SEE HIM! HE DROPPED A ROCK ON ME!

WHERE WAS HE GOING? THE CRAZY LOON!
OVER THE HILL TO LOOK FOR A LOST GOLD MINE!

BUT HE CAN'T GO OVER THERE! THAT'S A TARGET AREA! THEY'RE GONNA DROP A V-2 IN THERE ANY SECOND NOW!

IF THE MINE **WAS** HERE, SOME LOONY DOPE HAS FILLED IT UP!

UNCA' DONALD! **RUN FOR YOUR LIFE!**
YOU'RE GONNA BE HIT BY A **ROCKET BOMB!**

YES! THE ARMY'S TRYING TO HIT THIS TARGET WITH A V-2 FROM ONE HUNDRED MILES! THE BOMB'S ON ITS WAY NOW!

A V-2 COMING FOR THIS TARGET! OF ALL THE SILLY THINGS! NO WONDER TAXES ARE SO HIGH!

WHAT AM I ARGUING ABOUT? FEET, DO YOUR STUFF!
FROM THE VOID OF UPPER SPACE DROPS THE MOST AWESOME WEAPON EVER MADE BY MAN!
BULL'S-EYE!
THE EXPLOSION DIDN'T KILL ME, BUT THESE ROCKS IT KICKED UP ARE DOIN' THEIR BEST!

UNCA' DONALD! YOU'RE SAFE!
YES! YOU WARNED ME JUST IN TIME!

BRING ALONG ONE OF THESE ROCKS FOR A SOUVENIR, AND LET'S GET BACK TO THE CAR!

MILES AND MILES LATER!
YOU CAN SLOW DOWN NOW, UNCA' DONALD! THERE ARE NO MORE V-2'S BEHIND YOU!
GOOD IDEA! I WANT TO TAKE A BETTER LOOK AT THAT ROCK WE BROUGHT ALONG!

JUST AS I THOUGHT!

JUST AS YOU THOUGHT **WHAT** ?

THIS ROCK IS **GOLD**! SEE THE YELLOW STREAKS IN IT?
!
!

I KNEW ALL THE TIME THAT **OLD MAP** I FOUND WOULD LEAD ME TO **GOLD**!

WELL, WHY DON'T YOU KIDS **SAY** SOMETHING?
WE **CAN'T**, UNCA' DONALD!
WE CAN'T THINK OF ONE SINGLE, DOGGONE THING TO SAY!

THE END

DONALD DUCK
BY
WALT DISNEY
I'LL TAKE YOU KIDS INTO THE WOODS AND TEACH YOU ABOUT NATURE!
WE WANT TO LEARN ABOUT
BIRDS,
UNCA' DONALD!

THERE IS A BOBOLINK!
GEE!

AND THERE IS A CHICKADEE!
GEE!

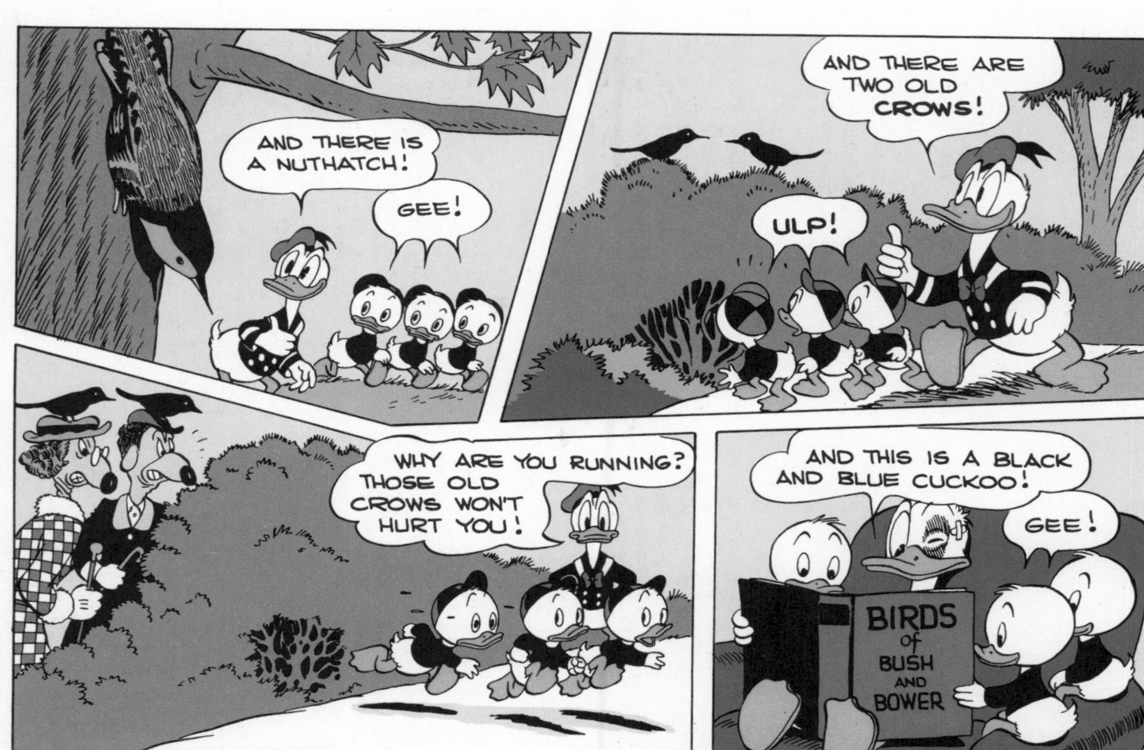
AND THERE IS A NUTHATCH!
GEE!
AND THERE ARE TWO OLD CROWS!
ULP!
WHY ARE YOU RUNNING? THOSE OLD CROWS WON'T HURT YOU!
AND THIS IS A BLACK AND BLUE CUCKOO!
GEE!
BIRDS of BUSH AND BOWER

THE END

DONALD DUCK

BY WALT DISNEY

WELL, WELL, A HORSESHOE! IF SOME JERK FOUND THAT, HE'D THINK IT WAS A SIGN OF GOOD LUCK!

THAT PROVES THAT HORSESHOES HAVE NOTHING TO DO WITH ONE'S LUCK!
LOOK, KIDS! A HORSESHOE!
SHALL WE KEEP IT?

NAW! UNCA' DONALD SAYS KEEPING HORSESHOES IS SILLY NONSENSE!

CLONK!

EIGHT DOLLARS FOR SEWING, AND TWO FOR BANDAGES, MAKES **TEN** DOLLARS YOU OWE ME!
I SEE I SHOULD HAVE KEPT THAT HORSESHOE!
Diploma
DOCTOR of CASCARA AND GALL PEBBLES

THE END

Walt Disney presents

Donald Duck

SURE, CHIEF!....YES!....I'D SAY IT WAS AN HONOR! I'LL BE RIGHT DOWN TO SEE YOU!

DON'T BE SILLY, SQUIRTS! ONLY BIG STRONG MEN ARE WANTED! NOT MICROBES LIKE YOU! GO PLAY WITH YOUR TOYS!
ZOW

UNCA' DONALD'S RIGHT! WE'RE TOO LITTLE TO BE FIREMEN!
YEAH, BUT WE COULD FIGHT LITTLE FIRES!
DON'T WORRY! SOME DAY OUR CHANCE WILL COME!

LATER
TO BLAZES I MUST GO! AND CHOP UP PEOPLE'S HOUSES IN THE EERIE BLAZES' GLOW!
DONALD DUCK

I'VE BEEN MADE FIRST HOSEMAN ON THE LADDER TRUCK... A POSITION OF GREAT HONOR!
13
LUCKY!
LUCKY!
LUCKY!

AT THE FIRST SOUND OF AN ALARM, I GRAB MY HAT AND AX AND DASH TO THE FIRE-HOUSE! THEN I RIDE THE TRUCK TO THE FIRE!
LUCKY!
LUCKY!
LUCKY!

FOR EVERY FIRE I ATTEND I GET A BRASS MEDAL, AND FOR EVERY ACT OF HEROISM I GET A LITTLE SILVER NOZZLE WITH GOLD HOSE COILS!
LUCKY!
LUCKY!
LUCKY!

I'LL TAKE THE STUFF OUT OF THIS CEDAR CHEST, SO I'LL HAVE A PLACE TO STORE MY TROPHIES!
MODEST, ISN'T HE?

THAT NIGHT!
OOOEEEE
OOEEEEE
DUCKBURG FIRE DEPT.

OOEEEE!
GAZAZZZ

THE FIRE ALARM
IS BLOWING!
AND UNCA' DONALD'S STILL ASLEEP!
ZZZZZZZ

WAKE UP, UNCA' DONALD!
THERE'S A BIG FIRE SOME PLACE!
GET UP, FIREMAN!

A FLIRE! A FRIER! I MUST SHAVE THE WOMEN AND CHILDREN!

WAIT! WAIT, UNCA' DONALD!

YOU FORGOT YOUR HAT!

THANKS, BOYS! I'LL REMEMBER THIS FAVOR!

WAIT! YOU HAVEN'T GOT YOUR AX!
13

HOW ABSENT-MINDED OF ME!

WAIT! YOU CAN'T GO LIKE THAT! YOU'RE STILL IN YOUR NIGHTIE!

DOGGONE THESE DELAYS! THE FIRE WILL GET OUT OF CONTROL!
13

I'M OFF!
UNCA' DONALD!

COME BACK AND PUT YOUR CLOTHES ON
BEFORE YOU GET
ARRESTED!

AT LAST!
HOLD IT, CHIEF! FIREMAN DUCK IS ON HIS WAY!

ULP! I'M LATE! THE ENGINES HAVE GONE TO THE FIRE!
HOSE CO. NO. 6½

AND THE FIRE'S CLEAR ACROSS TOWN! OH, ME! OH, MY!

WELL, NOBODY'S GONNA SAY FIREMAN DUCK QUITS TILL THE LAST SPARK IS OUT!

THE FIRE MUST BE JUST AROUND THIS CORNER!

LOOKIN' FOR SOMETHIN', BUDDY?
YES! THE FIRE ENGINES!

THEY WET DOWN THE HOUSES ALL AROUND AND WENT BACK TO THE FIREHOUSE! ANYTHING I CAN DO FOR YOU?
YES! CALL ME A TAXI!

NEXT A.M.
IT'S THE FIRE CHIEF, UNCA' DONALD! HE WANTS TO SEE YOU AT THE FIREHOUSE!
I BET HE WANTS TO APOLOGIZE FOR LEAVING ME LAST NIGHT! I'LL GO RIGHT DOWN!

LATER!
I'VE BEEN DEMOTED, KIDS! THE CHIEF MADE ME A SQUIRT MAN!
WHAT'S THAT?

WHEN AN ALARM BLOWS, I GRAB THIS HAND EXTINGUISHER AND RUN TO THE FIRE AND SQUIRT THE CHEMICALS ON THE FLAMES!
13

YOU MEAN YOU DON'T RIDE THE TRUCK ANY MORE?
THAT'S THE SAD STORY! I GO BY FOOT POWER! BUT I'LL GET BACK ON THE HONOR BRIGADE, YOU'LL SEE!

I'LL HANG THE EXTINGUISHER HERE ON THE PORCH WHERE I CAN GRAB IT IN A HURRY!

IF THE ALARM BLOWS TONIGHT, THERE'LL BE NO SLIP-UP! I'LL GUARANTEE THAT!

IN THE WEE SMALL HOURS!
OOEEEE!

THE FIRE ALARM IS BLOWING!
AND UNCA' DONALD
DOESN'T HEAR IT!
ZZZ!

WAKE UP, UNCA' DONALD!
THERE'S A FIRE JUST A FEW DOORS DOWN THE STREET!

A FIRE! STAND BACK AND GIVE ME ROOM!

MY JACKET!

MY HAT!

MY EXTINGUISHER!
13

ONE SIDE, EVERYBODY! FIREMAN DUCK IS ON HIS WAY!
13

THE FIRE ENGINES HAVEN'T ARRIVED! THIS IS A BREAK!

I CAN SPRAY THIS STUFF AROUND INSIDE AND PUT THE FIRE OUT BEFORE THE CHIEF GETS HERE!

SOMETHING'S WRONG HERE! THIS STUFF BURNS!

AWK! I GRABBED THE KEROSENE BUG SPRAY BY MISTAKE!

BOOM!

NEXT MORNING!
THE CHIEF IS ON THE PHONE AGAIN, UNCA' DONALD! HE WANTS TO SEE YOU RIGHT AWAY!

I CAN EXPLAIN THAT LITTLE MISDEAL LAST NIGHT! I'M SURE I CAN!

LATER!
WELL?
DEMOTED AGAIN?
UH HUH!

I'VE BEEN MADE A **WET-SACK MAN**! I GO AROUND WITH A WET SACK AND BEAT OUT SPARKS FROM SMALL GRASS FIRES!

POOR UNCA' DONALD!
WE MUST DO SOMETHING TO HELP HIM!

WE'LL BUILD A TWIG FIRE SOME PLACE
THAT HE CAN BEAT OUT WITH HIS WET SACK!

HERE IN THE ALLEY IS A SAFE PLACE!
BUILD A TINY FIRE THAT HE CAN PUT OUT WITH ONE SWAT!

NO! MAKE IT A THREE-SWAT FIRE! IT'LL BOOST HIS MORALE!

MEANWHILE!
A GOOD FIREMAN LOOKS OVER HIS OWN PLACE AND MAKES SURE THERE ARE NO FIRE HAZARDS ON THE PREMISES!

HA! HERE'S A CAN OF FIRECRACKERS THE KIDS HID BEHIND THE BARBECUE! THESE THINGS COULD CAUSE A HOLOCAUST!

I'LL PUT THEM IN MY POCKET AND THROW THEM IN THE CREEK SOMETIME WHEN I'M DOWN THAT WAY!

UNCA' DONALD, THERE'S A TWIG FIRE UP THE ALLEY! GRAB YOUR WET SACK AND SAVE THE CITY!

FIREMAN DUCK TO THE RESCUE!

TAKE THAT! AND THAT, AND THAT!
NOTE SPARK
SPLAT!

IT'S OUT! WHO KNOWS? I MAY HAVE SAVED A THOUSAND LIVES!

I SMELL SMOKE!

MY JACKET IS AFIRE! HELP! HELP!

HELP! MY JACKET'S AFIRE!
ROLL IN THE WET GRASS!
DON'T RUN INTO THE HOUSE!

THE FIRECRACKERS HAVE CAUGHT FIRE! WHAT'LL I DO? WHAT'LL I DO?
BAM!
CRACK!
POP!
WHAM!
POP!

UNCA' DONALD'S SET THE HOUSE AFIRE!
THAT ISN'T ALL! HE'S SET HIMSELF AFIRE!

I'LL PHONE THE FIRE DEPARTMENT!
I'LL ROLL UNCA' DONALD IN A BLANKET!
I'LL GET THE WATER HOSE IN HERE!

THE FIREMEN ARRIVE!
I'M THE FIRE CHIEF! IS THERE A FIRE AT THIS ADDRESS?
THERE WAS!
CHIEF

HMM! COULD HAVE BEEN A BAD FIRE, BUT I SEE THAT IT WAS CONTROLLED IN A COOL AND EFFICIENT MANNER!
YESSIR! WE WENT RIGHT AFTER IT, SIR!

YOU DID! AND HOW! SAY, I'D LIKE TO SEE YOU BOYS AT THE FIREHOUSE! HOW ABOUT IT?

LATER!
WE'VE BEEN MADE
FIRST HOSEMEN
ON THE LADDER TRUCK, UNCA' DONALD!

THAT NIGHT!
THE FIRE ALARM IS BLOWING!
OOEEEE!

OUR JACKETS!
OUR HATS!
OUR AXES!

FIREMEN NO. 13¼, 13½, AND 13¾ ARE ON THEIR WAY!

AND WHEN THE ENGINES ROAR BY....
LUCKY, LUCKY, LUCKY!

THE END